BE IGNITED

THE POWER OF ONE

31-Day Inspirational Journal

Inspiring, Igniting, Rewriting

DR. NEDRA L. BUCKMIRE

Welcome

When you understand the gifts of grace flowing in your life, you become intentional about how you release them.

As a voice called to '**speak life**' to:

- *Dead places so life can spring forth and thrive*
- *Dormant places that can be activated and begin to produce*
- *Broken places so they are healed and restored*

You show up and release your inherent excellence.

If I neglect to show up in the spaces and places where I'm graced, my gift of excellence fails to reach those it's intended to impact. Your gifts are meant to be exercised for the benefit of others. This is why '**Be Ignited**' has been released. Its intent is to **awaken**, **unleash**, and **activate dormant**, **dead**, **broken**, and **stagnant places** one word at a time.

The '**Be Ignited**' 31-day Journal captures the essence of God's heart expressed through mine. The inspiration for this 31-day journal was born as I celebrated each day of my birth month with a single word aimed at igniting others to action. Each day will provide powerful insights, empowerment, inspiration, biblical truth, and hope.

The power of a single word, or in some instances, two, can speak life and water dry and dormant places. Naturally speaking, any word spoken can either build up or tear down. Spiritually, what we profess can either **inhibit** or **free us**. Proverbs 16:24 declares, *"Pleasant words are like a honeycomb, sweetness to the soul and health to the bones."* Equally powerful is Proverbs 18:21, which states, *"Death and life are in the power of the tongue, and those who love it will eat its fruit."*

I want you to fully comprehend the depth of this scripture. In this context, '***death***' literally means pestilence, ruin, and destruction, while '***life***' encompasses being alive, living, vigorous, revival, and renewal. The vast contrast speaks volumes about the power we possess with our words!

- They can **empower** or **prohibit**.
- They can **inspire** or **diminish**.
- They can **ignite** or **extinguish**.
- They can **revive** or **destroy**.

As you journey through each day of the journal, it will inspire hope, ignite passions, and ultimately help you rewrite your future.

You may ask, how can one word rewrite your future? By allowing the word to realign your current path. If your current path, thoughts, and confessions don't speak life or reflect biblical truth, you will need to make adjustments. This shift can totally revolutionize your life and future.

In the **Be Ignited** 31-day Journal, you'll experience how the **power of one word** can transform your life. It is perfect for a morning, midday, or evening devotion. As you engage with each day, you'll have the opportunity to reflect on what the Holy Spirit has spoken to you, how the daily word has impacted you, and what you'll do to ensure your actions align with seeing lasting fruit.

If you knew your actions impacted another person's destiny, what would you do differently? This is the million-dollar question. Your actions, or lack thereof, affect not only your present and future but also those whom God has intended for you to reach. Whatever you need to do to **reflect** - assess your current state, **realign** - adjust your position as necessary, and **realize** - bring adjustments into concrete existence, act now.

Prayer

Heavenly Father,

I've been obedient to your word and direction in releasing what you've impressed upon my heart to capture within this devotional journal. I wholeheartedly believe your transforming power has been infused in every page. As your servant engages with each day, let the power of the Holy Spirit illuminate every word, concept, and admonishment contained within.

I declare the **power of one** will reach the depth of despair and discouragement and breathe new life. I declare every place of uncertainty will be assured by the power of your word. I declare every barren place is healed, and fruitfulness abounds. I declare weary hearts are revitalized. I declare every obscure place is overwhelmed with clarity. Let your sons and daughters walk in the freedom you secured on the cross.

We seal this prayer of victory over every reader. We stand in agreement that every reader will walk in healthy (*spirit, soul, & body*) places as they fulfill all assignments upon their lives.

Amen!

Day 1
RELEASE

Escape from confinement

2 Corinthians 10:5

Casting down arguments and every high thing that exalts itself against the knowledge of God, bringing every thought into captivity to the obedience of Christ.

The human mind's capabilities are vast. Yet, one negative thought can detrimentally impact the greatness of your mind's vitality. Our mind has the power to heal itself and, conversely, to cause harm. What have you allowed to dictate your thoughts and, ultimately, your life?

It's time to release yourself from every thought, expectation, opinion, agreement, and negative word you've aligned yourself with. An argument is any elevated place or thing that seeks to supersede the word of God. This release is **active and continual**; it's not a one-and-done process. It is vitally essential to escape from confinement because freedom is part of your inheritance as a believer.

Every restriction, whether self-imposed, intrinsic, or extrinsic, limits you from being uniquely who God made you to be.

Declare with me: I **RELEASE** every impediment that has held me captive. I am free!

Casting *down* arguments and
every *high thing* that
exalts itself against the knowledge
of God, bringing every thought into
captivity to the obedience
of Christ.

- 2 CORINTHIANS 10:5 -

TIME TO REFLECT:

What areas is the Holy Spirit revealing for you to release?
What will you do to remain free from what you've released?

_____

_____

_____

_____

_____

_____

_____

_____

_____

_____

_____

_____

_____

_____

_____

_____

_____

_____

_____

_____

_____

_____

_____

_____

_____

_____

_____

_____

Day 2
UNAVAILABLE

Not possible to get or use

Proverbs 4:23
Watch over your heart with all diligence,
for from it flow the springs of life.

When you make yourself available to a person, position, or thing, you open yourself to it with acceptance. There is an unspoken agreement due to the nature of harmony within the relationship. However, if something occurs to break the unity, a realignment is warranted. At this point, access must be denied. Our heart is the central controlling force of our existence, both naturally and spiritually.

If the connection drains you, you must become unavailable to it. This means you must be careful and take responsibility for your mental, psychological, and spiritual well-being. If it diverts your focus, remain unavailable to it. If it speaks lies concerning your future, shut it down. If it goes contrary to God's word, absolutely disallow it!

Declare with me: I am **UNAVAILABLE** to everything that separates me from my purpose, assignment, and place of grace.

Watch over your *heart*
with all *diligence*, for
from it *flow* the springs of life.

— PROVERBS 4:23 —

TIME TO REFLECT:

What people, places, and situations do you need to become unavailable to?
What will you do to ensure you remain unavailable?

Day 3
TIME

Measurable period which an action exists

Ephesians 5:15-16
Look carefully then how you walk, not as unwise but as wise, making the best use of the time, because the days are evil.

Time is infinite; however, the time you have been blessed with is not. If tomorrow never comes, what would you have done today? Whatever that is, do it now! Take immediate action because tomorrow is not promised. Proverbs 27:1 declares, *"Do not boast about tomorrow, for you do not know what a day may bring."*

What haven't you started? Perhaps procrastination has immobilized you. Or possibly, you've been comfortable. Comfort can become the enemy of the progress you desire. Remember, your passion is a product of your purpose. It's **TIME** to release what's in your heart and hands! How can you make better use of the time you've been blessed to enjoy and accomplish God's will?

Declare with me: I am a wise steward of the **TIME** God has given me. I will not waste the gift of today!

Look carefully then how you walk, not as *unwise* but as wise, making the best use of the *time* because the days are evil.

- EPHESIANS 5:15-16 -

TIME TO REFLECT:

Has time management been a challenge for you?
How will you ensure you manage your time wisely going
forward?

ACCESS
A means of entering a place

John 1:12
But to all who did receive him, who believed in his name, he gave the right to become children of God.

When you have access, it authorizes you to enter! **Read that again**. Possessing physical keys can elicit a sense of ownership and responsibility. Spiritually, your access is never removed, even if you don't possess physical keys. Whew!! Your authority flows directly from the power of the Holy Spirit.

This power is full, immeasurable, active, and guaranteed because of Christ's work on the cross. This is your right as a believer... **ACCESS**! Where have you been given keys to enter, and what have you done with them? I encourage you to maximize your access and walk in your authority. Do not waste the powerful privilege of access that was obtained for you. It's been given to aid you in taking dominion as God commanded.

Declare with me: I have **ACCESS** that has given me authority as a son and daughter of the Most High God. I will explore its full power and not neglect my privilege.

But to all who did receive him,
who *believed* in his name,
he gave the to *right* to become
children of God.

– JOHN 1:12 –

TIME TO REFLECT:

Are you fully utilizing your God-ordained access?
What will you do to maximize its power in your life

Day 5
ROADBLOCK
A barricade or any hindrance

Luke 1:37
For nothing will be impossible with God.

The word *roadblock* is naturally understood as an obstacle to progress. It's negative, an inconvenience, and can be extremely stressful. No matter how well you plan, everyone will face roadblocks. They frustrate plans and can cause major setbacks.

Unfortunately, they can create uncertainty concerning your present and future. Yet, roadblocks can be the breeding ground for invention and alternate opportunities. Yes! They can help you build resistance as you navigate through any challenge. I want you to be encouraged to know there are countless more roads than **ROADBLOCKS**. I implore you to look again and take the detour, as the roadblock could be a divine reroute!

Declare with me: I will change my perspective concerning every **ROADBLOCK** and open my eyes to the divine reroute in the detour. Glory!

For *nothing* shall be
impossible with God.

- LUKE 1:37 -

TIME TO REFLECT:

Are you currently facing any roadblocks, or have you in the past?
What will you do to shift your perspective and see the divine
reroute?

_____
_____
_____
_____
_____
_____
_____
_____
_____
_____
_____
_____
_____
_____
_____
_____
_____
_____
_____
_____
_____
_____
_____
_____
_____
_____
_____
_____
_____

Day 6
INFLUENCE

To affect or change someone or something

Proverbs 27:17
As iron sharpens iron, so one man sharpens [and influences] another [through discussion].

Our lives are influenced on a daily basis, whether we are cognizant of it and able to pinpoint its numerous factors or not. God created mankind as relational beings and is mindful of our relational well-being. If you've had the humbling experience of changing someone's behavior or contributing to the development of a person, a community, an organization, or a nation, you've influenced them.

Remember, influence is an absolute force, but I've learned it's not forceful! (*Holy Spirit inspired!*) It matters how you show up. Influence is defined as the capacity to have an effect on the character, development, or behavior of someone or something. Where have you positively altered the course of a person's life, organization, team, or group? This is the power of influence! Don't you dare stop sharing your genius. We need you.

Declare with me: I will positively **INFLUENCE** every life that crosses my path.

As iron *sharpens* iron, so
one man sharpens [and
influences] another [through
discussion].

- PROVERBS 27:17 -

TIME TO REFLECT:

Where do you desire to have a positive influence?
What will be your first step?

_____

_____

_____

_____

_____

_____

_____

_____

_____

_____

_____

_____

_____

_____

_____

_____

_____

_____

_____

_____

_____

_____

_____

_____

_____

_____

_____

_____

Day 7
AUTHENTIC

Of undisputed origin; genuine

Proverbs 10:9
*The one who conducts himself in integrity will live securely,
but the one who behaves perversely will be found out.*

Authenticity is vital in relationships with God and people. God already knows exactly who you are and still died so that you might walk in integrity according to His word. The origin of the word authentic is derived from '*authentes*,' an ancient Greek word which means '*one acting on its own authority*.' I'm thankful our authority is purified and purchased by Jesus' blood sacrifice. It stands on the power of the cross! Glory! This qualifies you and me to stand confidently with undisputed origin.

You are not an inferior duplication of an original. Any replication will mask your essential uniqueness. You were created as a masterpiece by God's purposeful design. Don't deny the world of your excellence. Be genuine. Be bold. Be uniquely you. Be of '**undisputed origin**'. You are absolutely necessary!

Declare with me: I am **AUTHENTIC** and created for good, distinguished, and honorable works! There is no one like me.

The one who conducts himself in *integrity* will live *securely* but the one who behaves *perversely* will be found out.

- PROVERBS 10:9 -

TIME TO REFLECT:

Have you masked your authenticity?
Declare below what God says about you!

_____

_____

_____

_____

_____

_____

_____

_____

_____

_____

_____

_____

_____

_____

_____

_____

_____

_____

_____

_____

_____

_____

_____

_____

_____

Day 8
WHOLENESS

The state of being unbroken or undamaged

I Thessalonians 5:23
May God himself, the God who makes everything holy and whole, make you holy and whole, put you together - spirit, soul, and body - and keep you fit for the coming of our Master, Jesus Christ.

Whatever broke you cannot hold you! Wholeness is available to every believer. It's part of your covenantal right. You must ensure you access every benefit guaranteed through Jesus Christ. When you are whole, your spirit, soul, and body are aligned, healthy, and fully connected to your inheritance secured on the cross. Being whole will cause you to see, speak, act, and respond differently. There is a completeness that can only be found in Christ's love for us.

If you are broken, you see through the lens of what broke you. I stand in agreement that every place of brokenness is made **WHOLE** and restored. You are free to act and do as the Father has made provision for you through Christ.

Declare with me: I am **WHOLE**. I am free from limitations that attempt to bind my spirit, soul, and body.

May God himself, the God who makes everything *holy* and *whole* put you together spirit, soul, and body and keep you *fit* for the coming of our Master, Jesus Christ.

- I THESSALONIANS 5:23 -

TIME TO REFLECT:

Where do you need to be made whole?
Declare your FREEDOM below.

Day 9
LEGACY

Something transferred or received from an ancestor

2 Timothy 1:5
I recall your sincere faith that was alive first in your grandmother Lois and in your mother Eunice, and I am sure is in you.

A legacy of righteousness is generational. In 2 Timothy, the first chapter, Paul recalled the legacy of sincere faith in Timothy's grandmother, Lois, and his mother, Eunice. Legacy goes beyond physical inherited items. It is something valuable you impart! Legacy leaves an enduring imprint upon every life it touches. How you live and conduct yourself in life can create a legacy.

Integrity, God-centered living, consistency, and perseverance are honorable characteristics. They are first modeled in the presence of people before they are imparted. An inherited bank account is a blessing. However, life principles that can impact present and future generations are priceless. What legacy do you desire to leave? What will it speak? What are you cultivating?

Declare with me: I will intentionally cultivate a rich **LEGACY** of honor, faith, and righteousness. It starts with me!

I recall your sincere *faith* that was alive *first* in your grandmother Lois and in your mother Eunice, and I am *sure* is in *you*.

– 2 TIMOTHY 1:5 –

TIME TO REFLECT:

What do you need to start, stop, or continue in order to be
intentional with the legacy you desire to impart?

Day 10
VISION

State of being able to see

Proverbs 29:18
When there is no prophetic vision the people cast off restraint, but the one who keeps the law, blessed is he!

What's your **D.R.E.A.M.** (*divinely realized expectation awaiting manifestation*)? What has captured your heart that you cannot release? What have you seen? All of these questions speak to what God has purposed you to see. It's His vision seen through your eyes. He desires for you to see and, ultimately, execute what He has revealed.

A vision can come from a divine moment of inspiration. It's the brilliance of a thought that can transform into reality. However, it will never be realized without a plan. It must be nurtured from inception to execution. God has given you a glimpse of His heart and desired plan for you when He shared His thoughts. I urge you not to let what you've seen and heard remain just a thought. Develop it from conception to reality! Capture it. Nurture it. Birth it.

Declare with me: I will execute the **VISION** God has graciously revealed to me. It was never intended to remain a secret. I will release what He has shown me.

When there is no prophetic *vision* the people cast off restraint, but the *one* who *keeps* the law, *blessed* is he!

- PROVERBS 29:18 -

TIME TO REFLECT:

What is your D.R.E.A.M. - *divinely realized expectation awaiting manifestation* (your vision)?
What is your first step to move from thought to execution?

_____

_____

_____

_____

_____

_____

_____

_____

_____

_____

_____

_____

_____

_____

_____

_____

_____

_____

_____

_____

_____

_____

_____

_____

_____

_____

_____

_____

_____

Day 11
AMPLIFY

To expand; to make larger or greater

Psalm 71:21
You will increase my greatness and comfort me on every side.

In our scripture, '*increase*' means to make large, enlarge, grow, and become numerous. It's synonymous with '*amplify*'. Do these words seem out of reach for you? God desires to accomplish exactly what He originally commanded for you to be and do. Within the divine imprint of our DNA, God created us to take dominion. Yes, dominion. We are meant to rule as His regents on the earth! You and I are meant to reflect how God rules—with integrity and sound decision-making.

To increase and become numerous, there must be something of substance to expand. What has God revealed for you to amplify? What does He want you to enlarge? What is in your hands? Remember, your excellence is purposed to impact others. If your excellence is withheld, it will never be known or increased.

Declare with me: I will **AMPLIFY** my voice and gifts to enlarge the will of the Lord in the earth.

You will *increase* my
greatness and comfort me
on every side.

- PSALM 71:21 -

TIME TO REFLECT:

How do you believe God desires to be amplified through you?
What's your first step to ensuring you are positioned for
greater?

_____

_____

_____

_____

_____

_____

_____

_____

_____

_____

_____

_____

_____

_____

_____

_____

_____

_____

_____

_____

_____

_____

_____

_____

_____

_____

Day 12
EXCELLENCE
Talent or quality unusually good; surpassing ordinary

Ephesians 2:10

For we are His workmanship, created in Christ Jesus for good works, which God prepared beforehand that we should walk in them.

It's within YOU! Yes, excellence is within you because the **Excellent One** dwells within you. It might be challenging for you to believe and accept this truth. Yet, it is true! You are Christ's own masterpiece, a work of art meticulously created before time began. You were already on His mind and given gifts before you came into existence. Please pause for a moment and digest everything the last sentence stated. Not only were you created in excellence for excellence, but there's also excellence within you. Glory!

What's your *je ne sais quoi*? What's your dominant excellence? Can you name it? Many may have similar qualities, but they will **never be you**. **Read that again**! You are magnificently created. When you can identify the absolute best of who you are, it directs you to where you're meant to thrive. Embrace your excellence and blossom!

Declare with me: **EXCELLENCE** dwells within me. I will reflect Christ's excellence through every good work.

For we are His *workmanship*, created in Christ Jesus for *good works*, which God prepared beforehand that we should walk in them.

- EPHESIANS 2:10 -

TIME TO REFLECT:

What's your excellence? Name it proudly.
Are you utilizing it to its maximum capacity? If not, why?

Day 13
HOPE

Expectation and desire for a certain thing to happen

Titus 3:7
So that being justified by his grace we might become heirs according to the hope of eternal life.

Jesus Christ is your eternal hope, providing a solid foundation to anchor your life. Your expectation should be rooted in the completed work of Christ and the infallible truth of the word. Without the cross, there is no hope! Christ's amazing grace is a precious gift.

His gift of grace unleashes your ability to dream again, allowing you to experience glimpses of your intended future. This is the power contained within a glimpse— it shares, shows, and speaks the heart of God concerning YOU. The glimpse produces an expectation for what you've seen. Don't ever stop hoping, expecting, and positioning to receive what God has spoken over you. Your **expectations + work** keep your dream alive! Keep hoping. Keep working. Keep believing.

Declare with me: I will not lose **HOPE**, for hope dwells within me. Christ is my hope.

So that being justified by his *grace*
we might become *heirs* according
to the *hope* of eternal life.

- TITUS 3:7 -

TIME TO REFLECT:

What are you hoping for?
Name your heart's desire in righteousness.

_____
_____
_____
_____
_____
_____
_____
_____
_____
_____
_____
_____
_____
_____
_____
_____
_____
_____
_____
_____
_____
_____
_____
_____
_____
_____
_____
_____
_____

Day 14
LOVE

An intense feeling of deep affection

John 3:16

For God so loved the world, that he gave his only Son, that whoever believes in him should not perish but have eternal life.

Jesus made the ultimate sacrifice; He became and took on all the sins of the world even though He was sinless. His purpose was to redeem mankind and bring them back to His Father. He suffered, bled, died, and rose with all power in His hands— all because of His love for us. There are not many people who would die for you, but Jesus did!

Love encompasses varied depths of emotions. At its core, love is the desire to give, often at the expense of oneself. Remember, one person can make a never-changing impact and forever change a life. This is what love does; it gives, covers, redeems, restores, heals, sets free, delivers, graces, and awakens. Love is a force that cannot be contained.

Declare with me: I am because God **LOVES** me. I will share His love as I share Him with the world.

For God so *loved* the world, that
he *gave* his only Son, that
whoever believes in *him*
should not *perish* but have
eternal life.

- JOHN 3:16 -

TIME TO REFLECT:

What has Christ's act of love produced in you?
What will you do to share His love?

_____
_____
_____
_____
_____
_____
_____
_____
_____
_____
_____
_____
_____
_____
_____
_____
_____
_____
_____
_____
_____
_____
_____
_____
_____
_____

Day 15
LIMITING BELIEF

Belief about yourself that restricts you

Luke 1:37
For nothing will be impossible with God.

Have you ever been tormented by the *"thought"* of something but had no actual proof of its validity? You allowed the *"thought"* to restrict what you were already *"capable"* of accomplishing. It taunted and arrested your abilities, hindering you from progressing beyond the point of the *"said"* limitation. **Read that again**! Our thoughts or perceived threats can immobilize us, rendering us completely ineffective. Do not allow unfounded thoughts that go against the word of truth to cause you not to stand in your authority as a believer. Remove every contradictory thought that attempts to elevate itself against the truth of the word.

Today, you will no longer allow a lie or belief that has no factual merit to paralyze you! You have the **power** to remove the limits from your heart and mind.

Declare with me: I am free from every **LIMITING BELIEF** that has sought to contain me. I will walk in the liberty won for me on the cross.

For *nothing* will be
impossible with God!

– LUKE 1:37 –

TIME TO REFLECT:

What limiting beliefs do you need to destroy?
Replace them with declarations of God's word.

_____

_____

_____

_____

_____

_____

_____

_____

_____

_____

_____

_____

_____

_____

_____

_____

_____

_____

_____

_____

_____

_____

_____

_____

_____

_____

_____

_____

Day 16
EMBRACE
Accepting something willingly

Ezekiel 3:10
Son of man, all my words that I shall speak to you receive in your heart, and hear with your ears.

There is a difference between being aware of something and personally receiving it. Anyone can acknowledge the existence of something without personally accepting its benefits. It's similar to reading the word but not embracing it personally in your life. The word is **alive**, **active**, and **sharper** than any two-edged sword. Yet, our failure to embrace its power suspends its benefits within us. **Please read that again**!

In our scripture, to *receive* means to take, lay hold of, carry away, or seize. Are there times you'll boldly declare the word and other times shrink away from certain passages you may cautiously feel you don't qualify? I want you to know that all of the word is to be embraced and lived fully in all of its power! The blood of the cross made you worthy. Embrace it!

Declare with me: I will **EMBRACE** the full power of God's word and not limit myself to what I judge I'm worthy to receive.

Son of man, all my *words* that I shall
speak to you *receive* in your *heart,*
and *hear* with your ears.

- EZEKIEL 3:10 -

TIME TO REFLECT:

What has stopped you from fully embracing God's word?
Identify areas within your heart that have influenced your
hesitancy.

Day 17
BECOME

Begin to be

Philippians 1:6
Being confident of this, that he who began a good work in you will carry it on to completion until the day of Christ Jesus.

An amazing work has already begun within you, as indicated by the scriptures. This work is a divine manifestation of the grace and goodness of God our Father, empowered by and through the Holy Spirit. Paul, the writer of Philippians, confidently declares that God's great work will undoubtedly be completed until the day of Christ's return. Now that you know Christ's work in you has commenced, what can you become?

You were created for more than just existing. What have you envisioned? What shows up in your dreams? What are your natural talents, skills, or gifts? These are often indicators that point you in the direction of releasing your purpose. However, to fulfill what you've seen, you must begin! As you release your purpose, you become what Christ desires. Christ is committed to you for all eternity. It's time to become!

Declare with me: I will **BECOME** all God has destined for me. I am essential, which is why I was created.

Being confident of this, that he who *began* a good work in you *will* *carry* it on to *completion* until the day of Christ Jesus.

- PHILIPPIANS 1:6 -

TIME TO REFLECT:

Where do you need to begin?
Declare how you will become.

_____
_____
_____
_____
_____
_____
_____
_____
_____
_____
_____
_____
_____
_____
_____
_____
_____
_____
_____
_____
_____
_____
_____
_____
_____
_____
_____
_____
_____

WORTH

The value of something

Luke 12:7

Indeed, the very hairs of your head are all numbered. Don't be afraid; you are worth more than many sparrows.

Your worth does not originate from a person, place, or thing. If it did, then when the person, place, or thing is gone, so would your worth. Nor is it founded on what someone has spoken about you. Remember, your worth can't be contained by the presence or absence of anything. If what you do (*abilities*) defines your value (*worth as a human being*), you'll feel a great sense of loss if you're unable to "*do*" what you've previously done. Your value is not defined by "*what you do*" but by "*who you were created to be*." Do not allow what you're able to "*do*" in any season of life to be the measure of how you see your value. You are so much more!

Your worth is unequivocally based on God's value system. He thought you were worth dying for and gave His life that you might live. **Read that again**! You are fully worth His death on the cross. Christ decided your worth long before you felt unworthy.

Declare with me: I am **WORTH** Christ's ultimate sacrifice because He made me worthy.

Indeed, the very hairs of your *head* are all numbered. Don't be afraid; you are *worth more* than many sparrows.

– LUKE 12:7 –

TIME TO REFLECT:

Does your worth reflect Christ's perspective?
Declare below what the word speaks concerning your worth.

Day 19
IDENTITY
The distinguishing character of an individual

I Peter 2:9a
But you are a chosen people, a royal priesthood, a holy nation, God's special possession.

Authority and access are naturally and spiritually connected to your identity. You are not just a mere individual; you are an heir of God and a joint heir with Jesus Christ. Never live beneath the authority, access, and privilege that Christ's completed work of redemption has bestowed upon you. Remember who you are. If you're unsure of your identity, your authority to function in any spiritual or natural capacity will be immeasurably limited. Your authority and access are inseparable from your identity. You are chosen. You are royal. You are an heir.

As a child of God, power and privilege are vested in you. Do not remain satisfied with not fully walking in the benefits of your covenantal rights. Knowing your identity identifies who you are, what you own, and what you are authorized to possess. It's time to renew your vision and take hold of what has been provided for you.

Declare with me: My **IDENTITY** has been secured. I will fully walk in its authority, access, and power!

But you are a chosen people, a *royal priesthood*, a holy nation God's *special* possession.

- 1 PETER 2:9a -

TIME TO REFLECT:

Have you fully embraced your God-identity?
If not, where do you need to make adjustments?

_____
_____
_____
_____
_____
_____
_____
_____
_____
_____
_____
_____
_____
_____
_____
_____
_____
_____
_____
_____
_____
_____
_____
_____
_____
_____
_____
_____
_____
_____

Day 20
RECLAIM

Retrieve or recover something previously lost

Obadiah 1:17b
*And the people of Israel will come back
to reclaim their inheritance.*

Your peace is priceless; protect it. Your voice is essential; use it. Whatever has been relinquished, lost, stolen, or buried can be reclaimed. To reclaim something lost, you must first recognize it has been lost. Just as the scripture states that Israel would return to reclaim their inheritance, you can recover what was previously lost. Are you in possession of the full authority of your right as a son and daughter of God?

What have you lost that you know must be recovered? Is it your peace? Is it the power to use Christ's name? Is it your identity? I encourage you to reclaim it now! If it's tugging at your heart, then it must be essential to your now and next. Do not waste another moment vacillating about whether or not to seize whatever has been lost. Reclaim it now!

Declare with me: I will **RECLAIM** my power, right, and privilege as a child of the Most High God! It's my birthright.

And the people of Israel will *come* *back* to *reclaim* their inheritance.

- OBADIAH 1:17b -

TIME TO REFLECT:

Have you fully embraced your God-identity?
If not, where do you need to make adjustments?

_____
_____
_____
_____
_____
_____
_____
_____
_____
_____
_____
_____
_____
_____
_____
_____
_____
_____
_____
_____
_____
_____
_____
_____
_____
_____
_____
_____

Day 21
PAST

Gone by in time no longer existing

Isaiah 43:18-19a

Forget the former things; do not dwell on the past. See, I am doing a new thing! Now it springs up; do you not perceive it?

Do not allow something that no longer exists to maintain influence in any area of your life. If it still negatively impacts you, consider it not relegated to the past. Identify, confront, and remove it. Reclaim the space it occupies for current and future wholeness. Our past can be sneaky at times, inadvertently creeping into our present day, attempting to dictate our feelings, behavior, and, ultimately, what we speak. This is a glaring indication that it's truly not the past.

It's time to release the past and embrace what God is doing right now. Every moment you linger in the past delays every new thing God has purposed to activate. Although the past may have impacted your experiences, it doesn't define your present and future. Let's identify, confront, and remove the things that negatively influence your present and seek to cripple your future.

Declare with me: I will release my **PAST** and walk in every new thing God has ordained.

Forget the *former* things; do not *dwell* on the *past.* See, I am doing a *new* thing! Now it *springs* up; do you not perceive it?

- ISAIAH 43:18-19a -

TIME TO REFLECT:

Do you need to release anything from your past?
What new thing do you need to embrace?

Day 22
MAKE ROOM

To clear space for something or someone

Jeremiah 29:13-14a

You will seek me and find me when you seek me with all your heart. I will be found by you, declares the Lord.

Clutter can invade both your physical and mental space, making it challenging to locate what you need or appreciate what you already possess. Whew! When clarity is absent, it hinders your progress. It is essential to clear space so you can see, hear, and pursue what you have made room for. To create this space, you must first recognize what is restricting your freedom. **Read that again**! Some restrictions are self-imposed, while others are external. Regardless, you need room to freely pursue what God has revealed to you.

Whatever holds value for you, make room for it to be realized! You are worth the effort to declutter and remove obstacles hindering your freedom and progress. Seek God with your whole heart and make room for all He has provided. Your deliberate actions will *'create space'* for a new season!

Declare with me: I will **MAKE ROOM** for every good and perfect gift that comes from Jesus Christ, my Savior and Lord!

You will *seek* me and find me
when you seek *me* with all
your *heart*. I will be *found*
by you, declares the Lord.

- JEREMIAH 29:13-14a -

TIME TO REFLECT:

Do you need to *'make room'* for your new season?
Declare below what you are removing in order to receive.

_____
_____
_____
_____
_____
_____
_____
_____
_____
_____
_____
_____
_____
_____
_____
_____
_____
_____
_____
_____
_____
_____
_____
_____
_____
_____
_____
_____
_____
_____

Day 23
DISRUPT

Interrupt an event, activity, or process

Proverbs 19:21
You can make many plans, but the Lord's purpose will prevail.

Have you ever planned a special event or trip? Everything is going wonderfully, and at the most inopportune time, something happens, causing everything planned to come to an immediate halt. This is an unwanted disruption. Most disruptions are considered negative; however, they can also be necessary shifts that alter your direction for the better.

A divine interruption causes an essential realignment along your journey. If it prompts improvement in any area, it is necessary! The initial response to a disruption can be stressful. However, not every disruption is meant to defeat you; it can propel you. **Read that again**!
Divine interruptions are ordained by God! However, God gets your attention; know that it's for your good.

Declare with me: I will embrace whatever God divinely **DISRUPTS** because it's meant to reorder my steps for His glory.

You can make many *plans*, but
the Lord's *purpose* will *prevail.*

– PROVERBS 19:21 –

TIME TO REFLECT:

Have you ever mistaken a divine disruption as an annoyance?
How did you recognize is was divinely ordered?

_____

_____

_____

_____

_____

_____

_____

_____

_____

_____

_____

_____

_____

_____

_____

_____

_____

_____

_____

_____

_____

_____

_____

_____

_____

_____

_____

_____

_____

Day 24
INHERENT

Existing in something as a permanent & essential attribute

Colossians 1:27
God willed to make known what are the riches of the glory of this mystery among the Gentiles: which is Christ in you, the hope of glory.

The ultimate sacrifice Christ made for your liberty, power, and inherent identity is an irrevocable gift! Once you accept Christ as your Lord and Savior, the benefits of your inheritance never expire. Your inheritance is imperishable, reserved, documented, and unspoiled—it's permanent! ***Whew... insert praise here***!

Christ in you is the hope of glory. God willed to make known the riches of His glory to you, enabling you to walk in His glorious, rich legacy. The moment you were spiritually born into the family of God, you were given a powerful spiritual heritage—a family name, family likeness, family privileges, family access, and family inheritance! Glory! I hope you are celebrating right now. The reminder of the richness of your legacy is breathtaking, permanent, locked-in, and divinely provided.

Declare with me: I am a child of God. Therefore, Christ's victory has provided an **INHERENT** inheritance.

God willed to make known what are

the riches of the glory of this

mystery among the Gentiles;

which is *Christ* in *you* the

hope of glory.

- COLOSSIANS 1:27 -

TIME TO REFLECT:

What does *'Christ in you, the hope of glory,'* mean
to you personally?
Has this perspective always been true for you?

_____

_____

_____

_____

_____

_____

_____

_____

_____

_____

_____

_____

_____

_____

_____

_____

_____

_____

_____

_____

_____

_____

_____

_____

_____

_____

_____

_____

_____

_____

_____

_____

Day 25
SOAR

To rise or increase dramatically

Isaiah 40:31

But those who hope in the Lord will renew their strength. They will soar on wings like eagles; they will run and not grow weary, they will walk and not be faint.

When you hear the word 'soar,' immediately, something or someone comes to mind. Were you part of what you saw? You may have excluded yourself from who or what you envisioned; however, God has not excluded you. Although this scripture's context speaks to weary people having difficulty imagining a new future, hope in God is universal and timeless! Hope in God is not confined to biblical stories; it's relevant for you right now! Hallelujah!

Just as Isaiah stated, all those who place their hope in God are guaranteed that He will **renew** their strength! I decree renewed strength over you today. I decree that you will **soar**! Yes, you will rise and increase dramatically.

Eagles are fearless, tenacious, and possess keen vision. So, soar like the eagle. I decree that the wind of God will breathe a refreshing over you, your vision, and the assignment upon your life. This wind will remove fatigue, frustration, doubt, and double-mindedness.

Declare with me: I will **SOAR** because I've placed my hope in God! He never goes back on His word!

But those who *hope* in the Lord will renew their strength. They will *soar* on wings like eagles; they will *run* and not grow weary, they *walk* and not be *faint.*

– ISAIAH 40:31 –

TIME TO REFLECT:

Do you believe you can soar, rise, and increase dramatically?
Where do you need to come into agreement with God's plan
for you to soar?

_____

_____

_____

_____

_____

_____

_____

_____

_____

_____

_____

_____

_____

_____

_____

_____

_____

_____

_____

_____

_____

_____

_____

_____

_____

_____

_____

_____

Day 26
PROCESS

A series of actions taken to achieve a particular end

James 1:12
Blessed is the man who remains steadfast under trial, for when he has stood the test he will receive the crown of life, which God has promised to those who love him.

Your process is working for your good! When you are in transition, a.k.a. *'process,'* it's crucial to maintain your focus. Whether it's a season of testing, personal, physical, or spiritual development, do not give up. Completing your process is of the utmost importance for your present and future. The process helps you see your areas of opportunity and strength.

Do not let your process overshadow your progress. **Read that again**. An individual's process to achieve a desired end or navigate through a test will vary. No matter how long it takes, keep moving forward! Your victory is on the other side of the process. Remember to celebrate milestones along the way because it helps you see what you have accomplished. Every believer can rest assured of the **guaranteed promise** of the crown of life when you've endured the test.

Declare with me: I will not abort my **PROCESS**! God is with me every step of my journey. I will succeed.

Blessed is the man who remains *steadfast* under trail, for when he has *stood* the *test* he will receive the crown of life, which God has promised to *those* who love Him.

– JAMES 1:12 –

TIME TO REFLECT:

What has your *'process'* taught you that you couldn't have
learned any other way?
How has your *'process'* strengthened you?

_____

_____

_____

_____

_____

_____

_____

_____

_____

_____

_____

_____

_____

_____

_____

_____

_____

_____

_____

_____

_____

_____

_____

_____

_____

_____

_____

_____

_____

_____

_____

_____

Day 27
EVOLVE

To develop gradually by a process of growth and change

Romans 12:2

And do not be conformed to this world, but be transformed by the renewing of your mind, that you may prove what is that good and acceptable and perfect will of God.

In order to evolve, three key components are necessary—intention, change, and growth. Living things grow, and growing things change. You've naturally evolved from the time of your birth until now. As a believer, there must be a continual determination to be like Christ. Therefore, your mind must be renewed. When your mind is renewed, there is a complete change in how you see, hear, understand, and live. It's in this gradual process that you are changed into another form. This is the biblical meaning of **'transformed'** in our scripture.

Christ's life and words **sustain** and **free** us. You understand that without a continual pursuit of the Father's heart and will, we will become stagnant. I encourage you to keep seeking, stretching, developing, and growing.

Declare with me: I will be deliberate in my development. As I draw near to my Father's heart; I will **EVOLVE** because His word transforms me.

And do not be *conformed* to
this world, but be *transformed*
by the *renewing* of your
mind, that you may *prove* what
is that good and acceptable and
perfect will of God.

- ROMANS 12:2 -

TIME TO REFLECT:

Have you been intentional to evolve personally and spiritually? If yes, how? If not, what will you do to become intentional?

Day 28
DILIGENT

Constant and earnest effort to accomplish

Proverbs 21:5

The plans of the diligent lead surely to plenty, but those of everyone who is hasty, surely to poverty.

Our English word diligent comes from the Latin word *'diligere,'* which means *'to value highly'* and *'take delight in.'* I can clearly see how the English word was derived from the Latin meanings. When you are diligent in a task, responsibility, or assignment, you take great care in how it's completed. Diligence is the absence of laziness and the embodiment of the continued execution of working on what God has revealed. As our scripture declares, being diligent leads to plenty! *(insert praise here)*

Biblically, plenty means gain and, figuratively, superiority, preeminence, and profit. Wow! I love it when biblical definitions speak **LIFE**.

Diligent work is rewarded. This helps you to know that your labor, consistency, and persistence are not in vain. God sees your faithfulness to what He has called you to complete. He not only sees but has provided His supernatural grace to divinely influence the outcome. Glory!

Declare with me: I will remain **DILIGENT** and walk in my ordained place of plenty!

The plans of the *diligent* lead surely to *plenty,* but those of everyone who is hasty, surely to poverty.

- PROVERBS 21:5 -

TIME TO REFLECT:

Where can you become more diligent?
Commit to two things that will help you in this area.
Write, plan, and execute them!

Day 29
LIBERTY

The state of being free from oppressive restrictions

John 8:36
Therefore if the Son makes you free, you shall be free indeed.

Liberty is part of your covenantal inheritance as a believer. As Jesus taught in John chapter eight, He shared that if the disciples abided in His word, they were truly disciples indeed. The continual dwelling, tarrying, and remaining in the word caused them to **KNOW** the truth. Biblically, know means to learn, to come to know, to get a knowledge of, to perceive, and to feel. None of this comes without remaining in consistent fellowship with the word of God.

When you **KNOW** the truth, it sets you **FREE**. This is the work of the Holy Spirit inspired through the word of God. There is no mistaking someone who is free, someone who once was bound, whether physically, emotionally, or otherwise. When the Son, Jesus Christ, the righteous one, frees you, you now possess liberty that cannot be denied! I stand in agreement with you today that you are free because the Son has set you free.

Declare with me, I will walk in the **LIBERTY** won for me on the cross! It's part of my inheritance, and I accept it.

Therefore if the son makes you *free*, you shall be *free* indeed.

– JOHN 8:36 –

TIME TO REFLECT:

In what areas do you need to walk in liberty?
Which biblical truths need to be applied to these areas?

_____

_____

_____

_____

_____

_____

_____

_____

_____

_____

_____

_____

_____

_____

_____

_____

_____

_____

_____

_____

_____

_____

_____

_____

_____

_____

_____

_____

Day 30
THRIVE

Grow or develop well or vigorously

Psalm 92:12
But the godly will flourish like palm trees and grow strong like the cedars of Lebanon.

When the Word of God likens you to a specific animate or inanimate object, it's vitally important to ascertain the origin of the comparison. In our verse, the godly will flourish (*thrive*) and grow strong like the cedars of Lebanon. The cedar tree is known for its firm roots, being uncommonly tall, wide-spreading, drought-tolerant, and not liable to decay. Yes!! It was used for building and adorning temples and royal palaces. Take a moment and ruminate on all the strength, resilience, and power represented in cedar trees. Whew! I'm praising God right now.

The strength of the cedar depicts a believer that's *thriving—a.k.a. flourishing*! In order to thrive, the environment must be conducive for growth! Listen!!! What environments are you currently in that don't provide space for growth? The righteous will flourish when they are nurtured in the right surroundings!

Declare with me: I will **THRIVE** because I am planted in healthy environments that are beneficial for my growth!

But the *godly* will *flourish*
like palm trees and *grow strong*
like the *cedars* of Lebanon.

- PSALM 92:12 -

TIME TO REFLECT:

How will you ensure you are in healthy environments?
What steps will you take to apply the biblical truth of thriving in your everyday life?

_____
_____
_____
_____
_____
_____
_____
_____
_____
_____
_____
_____
_____
_____
_____
_____
_____
_____
_____
_____
_____
_____
_____
_____
_____
_____
_____
_____
_____
_____

Day 31
EXECUTE
To carry something out fully

Hebrews 10:36

Patient endurance is what you need now, so that you will continue to do God's will. Then you will receive all that he has promised.

When God created you, He gave you some assignments to complete. Within the course of your life, you are meant to impact the world in a special way. Ephesians 2:10 confirms that we were created for **good works**. The Amplified Bible declares that *God prepared [for us] beforehand [taking paths which He set] so that **we would walk in them***. There has been a path set for you and me to discover and execute. Are you fully carrying out the plan God set for you? Your endurance is key.

I encourage you to discover what your good works are, create a plan, and get it done! Many find themselves simply existing and not fulfilling what they were born to execute, leading to unfulfillment because they are not releasing their inherent excellence. If you've procrastinated or didn't know where to start, begin with what God has already spoken. It's time to act!

Declare with me: I will **EXECUTE** the *vision/dream/idea* God has planted in my heart. It is meant to be released.

Patience *endurance* is what
you need now, so that you will
continue to do God's will.
Then you will *receive* all that
he has promised.

– HEBREWS 10:36 –

TIME TO REFLECT:

What requires your immediate action right now?
Identify at least two areas and specify the actions you will take
and when.

_____
_____
_____
_____
_____
_____
_____
_____
_____
_____
_____
_____
_____
_____
_____
_____
_____
_____
_____
_____
_____
_____
_____
_____
_____
_____
_____

Congratulations, you have completed the 31-Day Inspirational Journal! I believe you have experienced some perspective shifts and renewal, and have been provoked and refreshed along this journey. The **'Time to Reflect'** section is deliberate. We often read and sometimes don't apply what's been read. This purposeful activity causes you to connect what you have read to your current place in life and make adjustments in real-time. It is meant to assist you with capturing what you are experiencing to maximize the moment.

You have been **IGNITED**! A flame has been lit and must be continually fueled as you walk out your transformation. As a coach, pastor, and mentor, I love to give practical guidance to those I walk with to help them unleash their excellence. As you've gone through the 31 days, in order for what you've experienced to stick and stay, it must become part of your daily lifestyle. Here are six areas that will help you experience lasting impact.

- **Actively Engage**: It will be imperative to engage again with what you've been inspired to activate. Revisit your *'Time to Reflect'* responses to ensure that you are following up on and implementing what you have written.

- **Apply Knowledge**: Apply what you have learned. Take the examples and to-do items off the page, and incorporate them into your real-life experience. Practical application will quickly bring about the benefits you've gained during the 31 days.

- **Discuss and Reflect**: Discuss your newly-ignited insights with others. As you broaden your experience in what you are becoming competent in, it deepens your knowledge. Through discussing and reflecting upon what you've gathered, you can hear another person's perspective as it relates to their personal experience.

- **Teach Others**: Yes, teach someone what you've learned. As you become proficient with the newly learned concepts and paradigm shifts, teach them. You can assemble a small group of those willing to listen and learn. Teaching a new concept aids in solidifying the knowledge you have acquired and reinforces your learning.

- **Continuous Learning**: Don't stop at what you have written down to follow up on or execute. Continue to stretch yourself in all areas you've encountered as you embrace a mindset of continuous learning. Seek to expand and multiply your knowledge.

- **Practice Patience**: As you learn new information and revelatory content, it may take a moment to see it worked out in real-time. Be patient with yourself and allow the essential time needed for it to become an indelible part of your life.

These key areas will guide you as you create new patterns of assimilating your newly acquired knowledge.

I celebrate your completed 31-day journey. Remember, every new beginning starts with an ending. Welcome to your new season! What will you do with all that you've received during the past 31 days?

I invite you to stay connected with me on all my social platforms, via email, and my website.

Feel free to share your experience as you journeyed through the last 31 days. I'd love to hear what ignited you, inspired you, and ultimately helped you rewrite your future.

Let's connect!

 hopecoachnb@gmail.com

 www.linktr.ee/nbuckmire

Inspiring Hope. Igniting Passions. Rewriting Futures.

ABOUT THE AUTHOR
DR. NEDRA L. BUCKMIRE

Dr. Nedra Buckmire is not only a pastor but also a master certified life coach, mentor, and the Executive Director of the Ravens Hope Cambodia Mentor program. Additionally, she is the founder and CEO of Hope Fulfilled Life Coaching. Her unwavering belief in the inherent excellence of every individual reinforces her sole mission: to assist people in discovering, activating, and releasing their unique brilliance.

Functioning as a catalyst, Dr. Nedra empowers others to bring forth what has been assigned to their hands. Her commitment lies in aiding individuals to rewrite their futures, helping them realize, activate, and release their inherent excellence. Possessing a Bachelor of Arts in Leadership and Administration, a Masters of Science in Psychology, and an Honorary Doctorate degree in Theology from the School of Great Commission and International Bible Institute, Dr. Nedra's academic achievements reflect her dedication to personal and spiritual development.

Her life is devoted to inspiring hope, igniting passions, and rewriting futures, creating a lasting impact on the lives she touches.